CHRISTIAN REFELCTIONS IN TROUBLING TIMES

LIVING WITH COVID

Living with COVID began its life as '*How About This?*', a series of weekly reflections from pastor-scholar, Dr Bruce Kaye, to the suburban congregation where he serves and worships. Bruce's insights and practical guidance were and remain a great encouragement in a time of uncertainty and community apprehension.

With skill and grace, Bruce is able to 'take a read' on the mood of society and, through a biblical lens, fashion an apt and clear reply to our heart's cry.

I commend these short and pithy gems to the reader and trust they will offer much needed light and joy.

BISHOP STUART ROBINSON.,
Rector, South Head Anglican Parish, Sydney

Bruce Kaye has produced a delightful series of short reflections, covering a year in the COVID-19 crisis. Each piece is deeply pastoral, inviting consideration of key New Testament texts, along with prayers and examples from the lives of the saints, to help us as God's people to live out our faith in difficult times with patience, kindness and love. The reflections show a profound knowledge of the Scriptures, as well as sensitivity to the current context. It invites us to nurture our spiritual life, to love our neighbour, and to hold to our commitment to social justice. This is indeed a wonderful book for our times!

REV'D PROFESSOR DOROTHY A. LEE FAHA,
Trinity College
University of Divinity

One of the common themes I have appreciated over the years in Bruce's writings and talks concerns how we should live Christianly in the world and the circumstances in which we find ourselves. So it has been particularly helpful to read his short weekly messages to us as a church, during the COVID-19 season. He gently delves into this question of 'living Christianly' in the context of lockdown, the suspension of our normal human rights, the ethics of vaccine development, and so on.

Additionally, he challenges us to consider how we are able to look beyond our anxiety or loneliness, to find hope and patience through God's presence, and to respond to the needs of our neighbours and the wider community. In other words, these messages give practical suggestions as to how we continue to live Christianly during the challenges of the pandemic.

I have found them very enriching, both personally and as a basis for many a refreshing and engaging discussion.

ALISON KEENE,
A church member and a reader of the original texts

When Covid hit, the world changed, as did the way we do Church. Bruce Kaye's weekly column in our Church's *Community News* helped us to navigate the challenges of the pandemic through his practical Christian analysis and advice.
What a blessing his wisdom and spiritual insights were to us then, and now as we look back on the way God was at work through his people.

TIM MATTHEWS,
Managing Director, Triumph Communications

CHRISTIAN REFLECTIONS
IN TROUBLING TIMES

LIVING WITH COVID

BRUCE KAYE

COVENTRY
PRESS

Published in Australia by
Coventry Press
33 Scoresby Road
Bayswater VIC 3153

ISBN 9781922589125

Copyright © Bruce Kaye 2021

All rights reserved. Other than for the purposes and subject to the conditions prescribed under the *Copyright Act*, no part of this publication may be reproduced, stored in a retrieval system, or transmitted in any form or by any means, electronic, mechanical, photocopying, recording or otherwise, without the prior permission of the publisher.

Scripture quotations are from the *New Revised Standard Version Bible*, copyright 1989, Division of Christian Education of the National Council of the Churches of Christ in the United States of America. Used by permission. All rights reserved.

Catalogue-in-Publication entry is available from the National Library of Australia http://catalogue.nla.gov.au

Cover design by Ian James – www.jgd.com.au
Text design by Coventry Press
Set in Fontin

Printed in Australia

Contents

Foreword		7
Introduction		10
1	Being Good Samaritans	13
2	Hope in troubled times	15
3	The quality of patience	17
4	Respecting one another	19
5	Learning to be kind	21
6	Neighbour first!	23
7	We are not alone	25
8	Living Christianly	27
9	Growing personal coherence	29
10	Putting others before our church services	31
11	Faith beyond church	33
12	Letting go	36
13	Getting involved	38
14	Be serious!	40
15	Being Formed as Christians	42
16	Kindness and forgiveness	44
17	Gospel witness	46
18	Generosity in practice	48
19	Just do it!	50
20	Rumours and conspiracies	52
21	Relying on God	54
22	Being refreshed	56
23	Generous and kind	58
24	Take and read	60
25	The gift of music	62

26	Imagination and art	64
27	The face of God	66
28	The imitation of Christ	68
29	Authentic worship	70
30	Time to celebrate	72
31	Keep in touch	74
32	Daily prayer	76
33	Right or wrong	78
34	Our lives before God	80
35	Habits for Christian living	82
36	Church as collaboration with God	84
37	Influence and responsibility	86
38	Walking lightly	88
39	Resolution time and habits	90
40	Following Jesus	92
41	Heroes to inspire	94
42	Paul as hero	96
43	Difference and diversity	98
44	Things by the wayside	100
45	On truth-telling	102
46	Imaginative concern	104
47	Richard Johnson – chaplain in hard times	106
48	Moral choices and faith	108
49	Reflecting on our Christian narrative	110
50	St Patrick's Breastplate	112

Foreword

Bruce Kaye has written fifty short reflections for the electronic 'Community News' letter of an Australian Anglican parish church. One reflection was published each week from March 2020 to March 2021. It is a unique chronicle of an exceptional period of human experience and it conveys insights at a number of levels.

The COVID-19 pandemic began to take hold around the world in early 2020. The global impacts have been devastating in many places and severe almost everywhere. Australia has been lucky among the nations. Countless deaths have resulted. Hospital and health systems have been overrun. International and domestic travel have been nigh on impossible for extended periods. Tourism and hospitality industries have been decimated. Many businesses have collapsed. Many more are struggling to survive. Governments have spent huge sums in endeavours to stimulate economic activity, protect jobs and prevent recession.

In Australia, novel political dynamics emerged. An innovative 'national cabinet' saw the Prime Minister meeting regularly with state premiers and territory chief commissioners, in what heralded a new era of collaboration. We are left pondering, however, whether state governments exerted autonomy in their own interests, reneged on national goals, largely left states worst affected to fend for themselves and self-interestedly closed their borders to all deemed to pose a risk.

There has been devastation at the personal level, too. Frequent 'lockdowns' to minimise human interaction and prevent the spread of the contagious virus have required people to remain in their own homes for weeks and even months on end, unless engaging in some essential activity. Obtaining food, exercising or providing an essential service such as care for a vulnerable person or medical and allied roles were among the few reasons one could travel short distances. Police stopped and questioned people and fines resulted for being away from home for inadequate reason. People were prevented from being present for family weddings and funerals, medical emergencies and at the bedsides of dying loved ones. Enormous heartache resulted.

Community organisations, including churches, had to adapt quickly and they did. Livestreaming services, pre-recording and publishing on-line worship, devotional and educational resources commenced almost instantly and has continued. Meeting virtually on digital platforms became the norm. Clergy and lay people shouldered significantly increased workloads. Fatigue and burnout became evident.

All these dynamics lie behind, between the lines and sometimes come directly into view in these reflections. The collection constitutes something of a journal of individuals, families, states, a nation and a world on a difficult, uncertain and anxiety-producing 12-month journey. The journey itself continues and will for the foreseeable future.

This journey has also been a spiritual journey for many. It has tested the theological virtues and stamina of, among others, those who profess the Christian faith. Herein lies the focus and motivation of these reflections. They are offered

Foreword

to provide Christian people food for the heart and soul in navigating these treacherous times. If Christians are called to be 'light to the world' and 'salt of the earth', how then are Christians to live in the blight of this pandemic?

In the fifty brief reflections, Bruce Kaye draws deeply on his wealth of knowledge of the Scriptures and Christian history, on his insightful perceptions of global and Australian social currents and failures and on his long experience of the struggle to live ordinary life faithfully.

Here is food for the journey that is realistic, practical, hopeful and sustaining. It is a diet that promises to enable people of faith to manifest the fruit of the Spirit in daily life: love, joy, peace, patience, kindness, generosity, faithfulness, gentleness and self-control. Such a life, in such times as these, is a real gift to the wider community, as is this collection.

† Phillip Aspinall
Archbishop of Brisbane

Introduction

In mid-March 2020, the South Head Anglican Parish, Sydney, began to prepare for the coming COVID crisis. One part of the preparation was an expanded e-version of the Community News.

The parish minister, Bishop Stuart Robinson, asked me to write a short 'thought piece' each week for this new style COVID-19 Parish Community News. I was to offer some thoughts that might encourage members of the parish as they sought to live as Christians through this novel and different time. The series was offered under the title of *How About This?* – something to think about this week.

The column appeared every week for the following twelve months. *Living with COVID* is the compilation of those weekly articles. The Community News grew in size and style. It also grew in reach as more people from outside the parish subscribed to it. During the second wave of COVID in 2021, the Community News developed significantly along with a streamlined ZOOM version of church services.

My thanks go to Stuart Robinson for his initial invitation and constant encouragement. To Hugh McGinlay of Coventry Press who has been an amiable and inventive publisher. Marion Auld was the editorial organiser of the Community News and kept me on the timetable with generous encouragement. I am also very grateful for the many people who gave me feedback on the column and especially to my wife Louise who read every edition and enriched it with her comments.

Introduction

My hope is that this published version of the material will encourage people as we continue to work our way through this long running pandemic. For all of us, there is more at stake than just surviving; for Christians, COVID is an opportunity to test our faith and to grow in confidence in the gracious God whom we serve through Jesus Christ.

1

Being Good Samaritans

Jesus said to him, 'Go and do likewise'.
Luke 10:37

This last week has been critical for us in this country and across the globe. Here in New South Wales, social distancing has not worked that well. We were not practising it and apparently not taking it seriously enough. So, the government has tightened our living arrangements as they must if COVID-19 is to be restrained.

As I listened to the wail of ambulances rushing to St Vincent's Hospital, I reflected on what a contrast this is with the parable of the Good Samaritan. He did not call an ambulance – there were none that he could call. Indeed, there was not a medical profession or doctors or nurses. The ordinary person had to do what they could. Jesus' story is about responding to need. In his situation, you had to do it yourself.

We are in a very different situation. We have a world-class medical service that is staffed and able and ready to deal with this crisis. Being a good Samaritan means, amongst the more obvious things, helping those who are doing the job – the health and medical staff and all those who work in that system. They will be overstretched and this will be a long haul for them. They are the most exposed members of our community. If you know someone directly involved like this, encourage them. Call or message them. Leave a meal at their door. Let them know you are grateful for them and their work and that you are praying for them. They are the bushfire fighters of this challenge.

- Support those who are doing a demanding job for us.

- Let's not increase the work load of our health practitioner by our own actions.

That might be a way to be a Good Samaritan in this situation.

2

Hope in troubled times

*(Nothing)... will separate us from the love of God
in Christ Jesus our Lord.*
Romans 8:39

In his national broadcast last Sunday, the Prime Minister reported that there had been a drop in the growth rate of cases of the corona virus infection. This is good, he said, but there is a long way to go. Others hoped that this was a trend. Such hope is utterly understandable, but may be contradicted by the actual numbers as they emerge day after day.

This is a very fragile kind of hope. It is subject to a set of numbers that will go up and down. If we are to survive in a personal marathon of the kind we are living through at the moment, it will prove to be a very tiring even exhausting way to live. In fact, it will almost certainly have the effect of making our lives much harder.

We need a better way.

When Paul describes the situation of the Christian, he distinguishes between the hope we may have in regard to things in the here and now and the hope that we have given to us in Christ. We hope for what we do not see – 'the glory that is to be revealed to us'. With such a certain hope, Paul says, we wait with patience.

Patience will turn out to be exactly something we need in our lives at this present time.

Try reading these words from Paul each day this week and breathe it into your day.

> No, in all these things we are more than conquerors through him who loved us. For I am convinced that neither death, nor life, nor angels, nor rulers, nor things present, nor things to come, nor powers, nor height, nor depth, nor anything else in all creation, will be able to separate us from the love of God in Christ Jesus our Lord.
> (Romans 8:37-39)

3

The quality of patience

Love is patient...
1 Corinthians 13:4

In the last week, we have seen the disaster of the *Ruby Princess* now subject to a criminal investigation, northern beaches closed and physical distancing being enforced by police. The 'curve' seems to be turning and some are hoping that this will all pass by quickly – no chance. The Prime Minister says best outcome is six months, but no vaccine for twelve at the earliest. So, patience becomes the order of the day/month. Patience with the virus, the social systems, each other and ourselves.

You may recall Paul's great passage in 1 Corinthians 13 about love. First, he says it is the essential Christian virtue. When he begins to describe what love looks like, the first thing he says is 'love is patient'. In the Roman culture of Paul's time, patience was associated with valour and courage, enabling persistence in victory. Paul, on the other hand, speaks of patience as waiting upon God's provision in a manner that is appropriate for those who are disciples of the crucified Christ. It is the crucifixion that sets the tone for Christian patience.

The early Christians were very aware of patience as central to the Christian life. In the first two hundred years after Christ, there are more things written by Christians about patience than almost anything else. Of course, they were a minority in society and for some of this time they were a persecuted minority. Coping with overwhelming difficulty does not necessarily produce patience. We may put up with our circumstances in what we do. But our own inner thoughts and emotions may fight with our condition especially if, as with COVID-19, it carries life and death possibilities for ourselves or our loved ones.

From the very earliest times, as Christians reflected on the meaning of Jesus' death, patience has been central to their understanding of who they were as Christians. Patience, as an inner disposition that manifested itself in patient conduct, is part of our being Christians and seeing our lives in all their joys, frustrations and perils, as belonging to God who was made manifest in the crucified Christ.

This is a time to remember who we are and to treat the curve with the detached caution it deserves.

4

Respecting one another

Be at peace among yourselves.
1 Thessalonians 5:13

There is an interesting dynamic going on in our society as we live through this pandemic. As we are under pressure from the threat of COVID-19, for some of us the little things we used let pass may be a bit more aggravating, hang in the air longer. That's not just other people being difficult. It is also about how we deal with ourselves and our own responses – the loss of physical connection with extended family, the loneliness for those in single person households, the pressure of balancing home schooling and work obligations, the pressure on already challenged domestic situations . We are all different and it should not surprise us that pressure of sustained threat amplifies some of those differences.

The early Christians had great difficulty with the differences among the followers of Christ. At first, they thought that faith in Christ was just for Jews and it took some visions and hard work to see that this difference did not matter in Jesus' kingdom. The social distinctions between Christians caused serious trouble in Corinth and elsewhere.

At Thessalonica, the Christians had been persecuted from the very beginning when Paul founded the church there. This pressure emphasised differences within the community. Later,

Paul wrote to this church to encourage them. Respect those who work among you, he said, be at peace among yourselves, admonish the idlers, encourage the faint hearted, help the weak, be patient with all of them.

Be patient just as the crucified Jesus was patient in the face of brutal power. Patience shapes how we relate to others and how we treat ourselves when we are under pressure. That patience lies at the heart of who we are as Christians. It is how we should be with the differences that are becoming more prominent for ourselves and for others in this ongoing crisis.

5

Learning to be kind

Love is kind...
1 Corinthians 13:4

Over the weekend, the NSW minister for health issued an order that extended the reach of the spitting/coughing regulation to include not just health workers but all workers. This totally outrageous action was apparently occurring across the board in situations such as deliveries, supermarkets and shops generally. This phenomenon sent out into our society a ripple of anger and disgust.

Bad things send out ripples, but so do good things. Near where we live a small terrace house has put out a large open box on the front fence with packaged household goods and a notice saying that if you need something, please help yourself. There are multitudes of similar things going on in our society at the moment. Simple greetings to people doing community jobs delivering groceries; gratitude expressed to those testing people for the virus and to police doing a very difficult job; and gifts taken to hospital staff with a thank you note. These kindnesses also send out ripples of kindness across the community.

Because our circumstances are so different at the moment, and so constrained, it requires some imagination to find ways of being kind. But habits of kindness are worth cultivating.

Ripples of kindness do good things in our society. They grow richer social relationships, confidence in the character of our society generally and they help us to be better people. When Paul wrote to the diverse and sometimes disagreeable Christians in Corinth he told them that love was the greatest of Christian virtues. But love can mean a lot of different things. 'I am doing this to you out of love' may often foreshadow something quite unpleasant!

When Paul wrote to the Corinthians he therefore set out some of the characteristics of what he had in mind when he spoke to them of love. First, he nominated patience and then kindness. Our present circumstances give us a striking opportunity to learn kindness by doing kind things to others. In the process, we might learn to be better Christians. In our present circumstances as we are under a lot of pressure, some of us might also learn the larger challenge of being kind to ourselves. Love is patient, and love is kind.

6
Neighbour first!

Love is not envious...
1 Corinthians 15:4

The government has given us some good news this week. The number of cases continues to fall and they are looking at relaxing some of the constraining rules we have been living under. A survey this week showed overwhelming support for what the government is doing, but it also showed that some of us were finding the restrictions more difficult than others. There have been some objections to the physical distancing rules in relation to such issues as mental health and the isolation of the elderly in aged care. It is a very Australian thing that the location of the most public dissent has been the great beaches we so much enjoy or, as a government minister discovered, travelling to and from one's holiday house without some good reason under the guidelines.

It continues to be the case that the present crisis affects people in our society in different ways. Part of that is because of the existing, underlying inequalities in our society. Of course, for some, the sheer accidents of timing in our lives can make our experiences of the current crisis dramatically different. But these differences do not define who we are as human beings or as citizens.

When Paul tried to describe the character of love to the fractious and separated Corinthian Christians, he told them that love is not envious or boastful. There is a lot about boasting in Paul. The greater 'glory' you had in his society, the more you truly existed as a social being. Envy was the obverse of this boasting and together they defined who you were. So in Paul's society, you were defined by differences. In our society, we use different terms but this differentiating phenomenon remains.

When Paul says love is not envious or boastful, he nails the point that what truly gives our lives significance and defines how we should live is that we have been marked out by God's love in Christ. When we think of ourselves in that way, we are delivered from any bondage to our circumstances, to our social differences, and are set free to love our neighbours in their need.

In the present crisis, this kind of freedom can help us to be better Christians and put us in a better place to engage with whatever emerges in our society after this time of trial.

7

We are not alone

Draw near to God and he will draw near to you.
James 4:8

Learning to live with COVID-19 is a daily exercise. I heard of someone this week who said they had given up watching the news and the guidelines because there was so much they could not keep track of. I can understand that. There is a lot of news and advice coming through. Not all of it is given to us in a clear way by the media. Early on, there were a few instances of confusing messages from the governments, but not recently. The National Cabinet agreed a three step plan 'Return to Normality. States and territories will move at different times based on local conditions. National Cabinet will review our step progress every three weeks'.

This is not a menu as some media reported. The circumstances in regard to levels of infection in the states and territories are different. This is a clear national plan, not confusion or a collapse in national unity, as some media outlets announced. Clarity helps confidence and hope for the future.

The point is important because as our Chief Medical Officer, Dr Brendan Murphy, constantly tells us we are entering a very dangerous phase. Last week, we had good news about flattening the curve and truly remarkably low case numbers alongside astonishingly high testing numbers. This opened up some hope of success in this crisis and we felt like we could breathe again and relax a little. Not so! Our little ray of hope from Saturday whittled away on Monday morning.

When legal restraints are eased, it will be all the more important for each individual to keep to the physical distancing, hand washing, safe coughing, and staying at home and self-isolating where appropriate. These practices are to keep ourselves and others safe and to avoid a second and more dangerous spike.

But it is at just this point that as Christians we are challenged to live the life we profess. Our hope comes from God in the person of Jesus the good shepherd. From that enduring hope we can live with the changes in the natural hopes of our changing circumstances.

Let me offer you a prayer written by a friend in the United States.*

> Great shepherd of the sheep, grant that we may hear your voice this day. Where there is distress or anger or sadness, restore our souls. Even though we are isolated from all that once was familiar, gently remind us that we are not alone. Call us by name and lead us so that we may follow you into the world.
>
> Amen to that!

---

* The prayer is by the Revd Dr Paula Gilbert for intercessions at the Church of the Holy Family, Chapel Hill, North Carolina.

8

Living Christianly

Those who abide in me and I in them will bear much fruit.
John 15:5

We are now starting a new phase in the COVID-19 saga. Having flattened the curve of infections, we are now easing the social restrictions that have achieved that result. But these restrictions also have dramatically damaged or destroyed the working lives of millions of Australians and disrupted the social life of the nation.

Now we face the challenge of living through a much longer COVID period. It will be different and, in some ways, more uncertain because we will have to be careful not to allow a new spike which will almost certainly be more difficult to deal with. We may need to remember things learned in the recent past all over again. Social compliance will be much harder to achieve. How as Christians might we approach this phase? It will have to do with things we do instinctively. Social responses are more immediate and instinctive than significant moral decisions that we reflect on before acting.

When Paul wrote to the fractious Corinthians he made love the core character of the Christian life. He then described some broad stroke characteristics of this love – patient, kind, not envious or boastful or arrogant or rude. He then went on to more mundane habits of behaviour. It does not insist on its own way, is not irritable, or resentful. These are things that more obviously come out of our inner formed instincts without much thought or reflection.

In our ordinary social relationships, we don't usually reflect on these things. We just are them – resentful, irritable and insisting on our own way. These instincts are not learned by reading or cognitive calculation. Rather they are learned by practice, by formation. By the deliberate cultivation of Christian instincts. This is the shaping influence of God in our lives.

The very unusual situation we are in with COVID-19 provides a real opportunity to devote ourselves to the discipline of unlearning some of our social habits such as being resentful, irritable, and insisting on our own way. It may well be a challenging and disturbing experience for some. This is not a task to enable us to think more Christianly, but rather to be more Christian in who we are. Especially in our coming situation, being resentful, irritable and insisting on our own way are divisive habits that corrode relationships rather than build them.

Well-formed instincts will help us to cope better with the uncertainties of the new phase of the pandemic in a way that witnesses to the Christ to whom we belong.

9

Growing personal coherence

Anyone who comes to me I will never drive away.
John 6:37

Every week, there seems to be some change in the conditions of our living. This week we saw significant easing of restrictions on what we may safely do. More public activity in small groups, more possibility of returning to work and – most significant of all – our children go back to school. Of course, there are new challenges to face, like public transport and traffic systems. It will take a great effort in this area to sustain the early good signs this week. While we steadfastly comply to the government restrictions, will we perhaps think ill of those near at hand who don't comply. They are not socially responsible. Why should I comply when others don't?

It might be helpful to notice something from the great Swiss psychologist, Paul Tournier. He made a distinction between our 'persona' – who we present to the outside world, and our 'person' – who we are to ourselves in our private thoughts and feelings. We all have and need a private world. But as this pandemic grinds on, a distance can begin to emerge between our person and our persona. Paul Tournier said that when these two become really distinct and different, it can sometimes be a factor in emerging psychological distress. In our current situation, this distinction can be amplified for some by social isolation.

For Christians, there is a special point here. We believe that our lives are open to God and fully known and understood by him and that is what is ultimately important. Furthermore, because God in Christ is present to us in grace and love, this offers encouragement and hope to the Christian. That divine presence is, of course, something we need to embrace for ourselves. In this circumstance there are things we can do as Christians to shape ourselves by that grace of God.

The apostle Paul, again with the fractious Corinthians, told them that love does not rejoice in wrongdoing but rejoices in the truth. Making a habit of not rejoicing in wrongdoing of whatever kind, is like feeding our inner person and nourishes us as whole and coherent people. Feeding our inner person by rejoicing in the truth of God's love for us in Christ strengthens us as whole and coherent people. Our persona and our person become more coherently connected and give us inner strength and outer confidence.

When we are such people, we not only witness in our lives to Christ, but we are also better citizens, more able to contribute to the protection of our society in the face of the COVID scourge.

10

Putting others before our church services

... so that we may be mutually encouraged by each other's faith.
Romans 1:12

Yet another step in our COVID-19 experience. Schools are back, but not without some problems, with two schools in the eastern suburbs being closed immediately because of a single infection in each school. New rules about church gatherings have been issued, although their accompanying guidelines were not published at the same time. It seems that fifty people might be able to gather in a place of worship, but social distancing will apply and a record (name, address and phone number or email) for those attending will need to be kept for infection tracking. These further details make it clear that this is a very cautious relaxation.

Our public health authorities keep reinforcing the truth that this dangerous virus is still at large in the community and that we need to be ready for a second wave of infection.

In these circumstances, Christians should reflect carefully on what we actually want to show to our fellow citizens in this crisis. What actions should the churches take that might say something Christian to the community? How should we individually live in these circumstances? What should our witness be in this loosening and fraught situation?

May I again refer to Paul's description of love for the fractious Corinthians. He tells them in their enthusiasm, that love bears all things, believes all things, hopes all things, endures all things. These are words of patience and endurance. They do not suggest energetic activity to the Corinthians whose gatherings were notoriously energetic. In this particular context, Paul describes love in 'quieter' terms, gaining resilience by being part of the Christian hope and thus enabling Christians to endure.

There is no life threatening reason for Christians in our present circumstances to resume gatherings in our church buildings and certainly not pressing the government for special privileges. Christians here and elsewhere have been remarkably inventive in sustaining their communities in recent months, whereas sadly a church service in Frankfurt was the cause of an outbreak of COVID-19 which affected over a hundred people. What witness would we like to leave as our heritage in these circumstances – enthusiastic and early resumption of church services, or a response of caution, putting the safety of our neighbours ahead of ourselves?

As Christians, we are people who belong to Christ and live according to his kingdom and so live by words of patience and endurance. Now is a good time for each of us and for the churches generally to live that way. We should not be jockeying for early privileges in seeking return to church. We should put our neighbours first and wait.

11

Faith beyond church

Love does no wrong to a neighbour...
Romans 13:10

Can you believe that it is exactly three months since the Commonwealth Government banned travel from China? This is number 11 of 'How About This,' which began the day after the government declared a national human biosecurity emergency on 17 March 2020. Just under three months later, we are experiencing the first stages of restriction easing, though our health authorities warn us that the worst may be still to come. It all depends on whether we have a second or third wave of infection. It is an important time in which we have the opportunity to think about how best as Christians to approach this easing situation in our own particular setting as citizens.

But this is also a time to be thinking about those wider issues that confront us as a community. One of those issues has been forced into our foreground by the protests that have convulsed and disrupted the US following the killing of George Floyd. The US reaction crossed the Pacific very quickly. This was not just because of the effectiveness of social media; more importantly, here in Australia, there was a rich soil of frustration about the high rate of imprisonment and deaths in custody of our indigenous people. Added to this was the video of an assault on an indigenous man by a Sydney policeman. This was only the latest in a long history of doing wrong to our indigenous neighbours in this country.

The result was that we were torn between two vital public issues – Aboriginal deaths in custody and public safety from the COVID-19 pandemic. We did not have a riot or civil disorder, as happened in the USA – quite the contrary. It would be a great mistake, however, to imagine that either of these challenges will go away.

Might it be that, having escaped the most disastrous health outcomes of this pandemic, and in many cases having found new ways of living, we might also find new resolve and imagination to listen to and work with our indigenous neighbours to set right the wrongs of the past which continue into the present?

When the Apostle Paul wrote to the Christians in Rome, a group he had never met, he told them something very important: 'love *does* no wrong to a neighbour'. Part of loving our neighbour is not doing wrong to them. On any reckoning we, as a community, are doing wrong to our indigenous neighbours as they encounter the legal and judicial system in our state. The relevant laws are mostly state laws and under state authorities. Not everyone can walk the streets in protest. Not all are church leaders with a public presence. Christians are not called to do what they cannot do. But a faith that is simply personally individualistic or church focused has only a limited claim to the title Christian.

Coming out of the COVID crisis provides an opportunity for us to come out of our personal and ecclesial world and engage with the wrong done, and continuing to be done, to our indigenous neighbours. Perhaps it is time for us – as churches and as individual Christians – to look at the other side of our good Samaritan obligations to care for our neighbour. Time to reckon with the wrong being done and to take up Paul's injunction – 'love does no wrong to a neighbour'. In our situation, that surely means that we should stop doing wrong to our indigenous neighbours.

12

Letting go

... not my feet only but my hands and my feet.
John 17:9

As we make our way into the easing of restrictions to prevent the spread of COVID-19, we are running into some ups and downs and also into a slightly different place. The large public protest gatherings were a bit of a downer for social distancing and the health advice, and thus increased the risk of higher infection rates. We had more cases this week that have arisen from lawful actions under the easing steps. Schools have run into a few problems. Imagine suddenly having to close a school and send all the children home and then 'deep clean' the whole school.

In some sense, the present challenges are now more personal. There is easing allowed but there is now more room for us to make our own judgment about how far to act on these freedoms. So unless we follow the responsibility-denying line of whatever is lawful is right to do, we now have to take more responsibility for our COVID-19 decisions. More responsibility is often a bit scary and our general low morale can get a bit worse.

For Christians, there is the great assurance of God's love for us in Christ but even light depression can drive such truth out of sight. That can easily be a question for us, especially in testing times, and these are certainly testing times.

In our present situation, one way to approach this would be to recall – in an act of reflective imagination – a story from the New Testament documents. John 13:1-20 describes the first thing Jesus did at his last supper with the disciples – he washed their feet. Find a quiet time and place – as much as you can – then read the passage in John. Visualise the scene: who was there and what happened, step by step. Then identify with one of the people in the story and put yourself in their position in the story. Re-read the story imagining how you experienced the event. How did those around 'you' feel at the time? Be reminded of God's presence in Jesus' ministry and lay your life before God in prayer. Don't ask for anything. Just be there.

In the ups and downs of our present circumstances, regular focused meditation might be a good way to maintain our resilience and develop our capacity to live more consciously in the presence of God.

13

Getting involved

He bandaged his wounds, having poured oil and wine into them.
Luke 10:34

It has been hard in the last weeks not to be aware of the terrible conflict of choices that has divided people in our country. On the one weekend, we had two major public protests about our treatment of indigenous Australians and of refugees. The events were confronting for their rejection of social distancing health rules, giving higher priority to the current and historic treatment of indigenous people in Australia and the treatment of refugees and asylum seekers in our country. Church voices were noticeably absent from the public debate.

In Australia, there appears to be some light in the covid experience, though certainly not elsewhere. We do not yet have full social freedoms but, little by little, more is possible, at least for the moment. So this might be a time to think about and imagine the future.

What might we plan to do when we are able to act more freely? I think one of the things we could do is learn a lesson about priorities from the two protests. They point to two of the most profound social failures in our society, one with a long and bitter history and the other with a short and harsh history. Christians have been involved in protests, campaigns and contributing to both issues but in general the situation is still very bad. Contributing to a movement to change our nation's approach to these two issues might be a good thing to plan for.

In relation to our treatment of indigenous people, we probably need to learn some history. Over the years, I have read a number of books on this topic. My current read – *Dark Emu* by Bruce Pascoe – suggests a wholly different way of thinking about our history. Though very popular, this book has not won academic support on a number of fronts. However, while details may not always be correct, the overall story is both challenging and illuminating.

The same could be said of Geoffrey Blayney's 1976 publication *Triumph of the Nomads, A History of Aboriginal Australia*. Despite criticisms, both books raise a set of vital questions.

One of the sad things is that serious scholarly work has been going on in this area for fifty years but has not won much public attention. Since 1977, the Australian National University has published the *Aboriginal History Journal* and this provides a record of high level, scholarly work.

If you think of learning about our past in this area, may I suggest the following:

Bill Gammage, *The Biggest Estate on Earth. How Aborigines made Australia* or Stephen Gapps, *The Sydney Wars*.

Some guides are given on the very helpful ABC web page https://www.abc.net.au/triplej/programs/hack/here-are-10-positive-ways-to-engage-with-indigenous-issues/10885222

It may be time for some different reading and planning for public witness as Christians in this great south land with its hidden history of indigenous people.

14

Be serious!

You have the words of eternal life.
John 6:68

The news this week has not been good. COVID cases across the world are increasing rapidly but major nations are relaxing restrictions. It has become possible to think that we are seeing the eclipse of US super power pre-eminence, to wonder what on earth is going on in Europe and what might happen yet in India, Africa or South America. Good news in Australia is challenged by the spike in Victoria – their second and larger spike. Now there are more restrictions with vast and focused testing.

Australian journalism's elder statesman, Paul Kelly, wrote over the weekend, 'The road to combating COVID-19 is getting longer and steeper. The strains on individual psychology and fortitude will intensify'. The effects of this pandemic are going to be with us for a generation. We don't need just the capacity to get to the next apparent point of relief, such as opening people-present church events or the flattening of the Victorian infection rates. We need to find ways of living in the longer run. That means not just ways of surviving but ways of flourishing.

As Christians, that must mean figuring out ways of living Christianly in these conditions. That means walking in the steps of the apostles, as people who belong to God in Christ and live out the terms of that relationship. It used to be said that we know God's presence through word and sacrament, but we should remember that these are not in themselves the presence of Christ, but means for us to enter into and be shaped by that presence. Because of our inherited tradition, Anglicans don't have much access to the sacrament of Holy Communion, though that might change in time.

We should never forget that our faith is in Christ and that Jesus Christ came in a particular historical time and place. The documents of the New Testament take us back into the life of Jesus and the experience of the disciples and the earliest generation of Christians. Delving into these documents and entering into that first generation's life is a vital part of knowing and growing in our own lives as Christian people. That delving is a bit like a gardener regularly tending and watering their garden to grow the seeds that have been planted. The flowers of this garden are the Christian qualities of our living, or in Paul's own gardening image – the fruit of the Spirit.

Over the coming weeks, I will try to write about various aspects of this challenge in order to explore what a longer-term strategy might involve.

15

Being Formed as Christians

Strive first for the kingdom of God.
Matthew 6:33

This has been quite a big week. COVID-19 has come back to Victoria with a vengeance. Our thoughts and prayers go out to those poor people in the nine towers who are subject to all the awful conditions of a strict lockdown. All State and Commonwealth authorities have been in an absolutely terrible position. They have had to make decisions of truly momentous significance for so many people in response to constantly changing circumstances. They can't expect to get it absolutely right. They can only do as well as they can in the circumstances.

On a much more modest scale, Christians are in a similar situation. Christians live on the basis of their relationship to God in Christ and in the context of their apprehension of the actual circumstances in front of them. That requires at least two things – a moral compass that can distinguish what is Christianly important in the context and some sense of what they can actually do as a Christian in that situation. Such decisions are not always clear cut, especially where there is confusion or lack of clarity about what is at stake.

Jesus' immediate followers were called disciples, a word with a clear connotation of learning. Jesus spent a lot of time teaching his disciples; some theology and its moral character. The disciples were being formed for the way they were to live. We can see in Paul's letters how he tries to shape the next generation in a similar way. They were being formed as Christian people so that their lives might be an expression of the moral character of the kingdom of God. They were being trained so that they developed Christian character. It was a slow process.

Ever since, Christians have been in the same situation. We need to be formed in Christian character. This is a bit like being trained to have spiritual/moral muscle memory. So that when we are faced with significant decisions we can perceive and act Christianly. This is not just ethics. This is a life that is lived in the presence of God and inspired by the Holy Spirit. It therefore expresses the moral character of the kingdom of God.

The key to living Christianly is having formed instincts or character that enable some insight and strength to act Christianly in challenging circumstances. We live in the kingdom of God and are called to live as citizens of that kingdom, but we can't expect to get it absolutely right. We can only do as well as we can in the circumstances.

16

Kindness and forgiveness

Be kind to one another, tenderhearted, forgiving one another.
Ephesians 4:32

It has not been a great week in Victoria, nor indeed if you patronise the *Crossroads Hotel* in Casula. I find it hard to get out of my mind the drawn but doggedly determined face of Daniel Andrews announcing more bad news in Victoria or Gladys Berejiklian with her worried demeanour and patient sticking at the task. These and other servants of our commonwealth have been bearing unfathomable burdens and taking hugely responsible decisions in highly complicated circumstances. COVID-19 is a moving target and they are responding to fresh challenges every day. It is inevitable that some things will go wrong.

We also face challenges about how we approach our own living in such ambiguous times. How far to go out. How to protect ourselves, care for others, fulfil our work or social obligations. At the end of the ABC program *The Drum*, the host Julia Baird farewelled viewers with the words, 'Wash your hands, be kind and stay safe'.

It is good advice but I think as Christians we can say more. Kindness is one of the pre-eminent virtues of the Christian life. In Ephesians, Paul puts kindness at the very peak of importance when he declared that the whole history of salvation was to show the 'immeasurable riches of his grace in **kindness** towards us in Christ' (Ephesians 2:7). And in Colossians, he includes **kindness** as part of the fruit of the Spirit and so he makes it a challenge for Christians; 'As God's chosen ones, holy and beloved, clothe yourselves with compassion, **kindness**, humility, meekness and patience' (Colossians 3:12). This is a call to be Christian – Christ-like in how we behave ourselves.

As the COVID-19 crisis continues, we will have reached a stage when church services on site will re-commence. Like other things in this crisis, as we have seen with government responses, we cannot assume that it will be all smooth sailing. There will be bumps along the way and mistakes will be made. We will not necessarily all agree with each other about what the parish should do or what has been done. These decisions are taken by those in our community to whom such responsibility is given and they will continue to do the best they can in very difficult circumstances. That is all we can ask of them. Much more important than the details of these decision, or our individual decisions in this matter, is how we conduct ourselves.

If we all clothe ourselves through this period with compassion, **kindness**, humility, meekness, and patience, then we will have done well as a Christian community and that is what is most important.

17

Gospel witness

*Mary Magdalene went and announced to the disciples,
'I have seen the Lord'.
John 20:18*

Pope John Paul II canonised more saints in the Roman Catholic Church than all his predecessors together. He said that we need heroes who come from our own societies to look up to and be inspired. In the Anglican Church, we tend to restrict the number of saints/heroes we remember. In our APBA prayer book, we have more women and a number of Australians for whom there is a day. In this time of the year, our prayer book gives us a number of such saints to remember. This week two are noted. Mary Magdalene (22 July) and James the Apostle (25 July).

Here are couple of things about these two Christians that might be worth reflecting on in our present complicated and difficult circumstances.

Mary Magdalene simply means she came from Magdala in Galilee, a small town by the Sea of Galilee. She was among a group of women who had been healed by Jesus and who then accompanied Jesus and his disciples providing them with resources (Luke 8:1-3). She is among a further number of women present at the crucifixion and had a key role in identifying Jesus' resurrection and the completion of his earthly ministry. She is a wonderful example of restoration and openness to a greater narrative than was immediately apparent in the unfolding events. Perhaps the challenge to us is also to hold ourselves open to God's greater narrative and to see behind the vicissitudes of our daily life the spirit of a gracious God.

James the apostle was a key player in Jesus' ministry and in the early church. He and his brother responded immediately to Jesus' call to discipleship leaving behind family and future security. They were a wilful and wrong-headed pair (Mark 3:17, 10:39) and were given the nick name of Boanerges (sons of thunder); but they were faithful and fearless and for this James paid with his life at the hands of Herod Agrippa I (Acts 12:2).

Mary Magdalene – forgiven and healed and knowing God in the power of Jesus' risen life.

James – impulsive and enthusiastic follower of Jesus, with a lot to learn.

In their different ways, they were open to God and determined to be genuine disciples of Jesus – heroes to challenge and inspire.

18

Generosity in practice

Give and it will be given to you.
Luke 6:38

COVID-19 continues scything its way through the world and in Australia through Victoria –more people dying, more people being tested and significant numbers not found after testing. Then the Treasurer, Josh Frydenberg, delivered 'mouth-watering' figures of financial stress for years to come. Then an infection centre at a church in Sydney. It is not good and these are very testing times.

But they are more testing for some than others. There has been a steep increase in domestic violence, there are more people seeking financial help, people normally just coping, now in COVID cannot manage at all. Existing disadvantage is magnified by this crisis. As Christians, we are committed to helping the needy, whatever that need is. Paul reports that the churches in Greece sent funds to the church in Jerusalem when they were in need. In Thessalonica, the church had a welfare system for those in need. After Pentecost, the Jerusalem church went for a form of communal property but it caused trouble, did not really work and disappeared from the record.

How we respond to the need depends on the circumstances. In our present situation, most of us would cause more trouble than good working alongside health workers or others on the frontline of the community's fight against COVID.

So we probably need to think of contributing indirectly. What might that look like? Perhaps we could see where some of the pressure points are and find an agency through which we can make a contribution – volunteering, donating, encouraging. Different needs and agencies need different things so we each need to figure out what we can realistically do.

How about thinking about it this way? Before COVID, there was already serious suffering in a number of areas in our society. These problems have all got worse under COVID. Think about the critical rise in domestic violence under COVID, or poverty for long-term unemployed, for the disadvantaged, for single parent families or indigenous groups. So identify our own priority list and select an area and search out a relevant agency and support them in whatever way we can. The project described in the *Bulletin for the Asylum Seeker Centre* would be a good place to start.

We cannot do everything, but we can do something.

19

Just do it!

Be careful how you live... make the most of the time.
Ephesians 5:15

What a COVID week this has been. Last week, the world reached just under 18 million cases and 682,000 deaths. Last week, the Australian national death toll reached 201, 46 of these occurred in the last week. Victoria has reached 116, 93 of which occurred in the month of July. We watch the figures and hope that the Victorian surge is perhaps peaking, and that the second wave in NSW is not eventuating. But we have been warned from the beginning that second third and fourth waves are almost certain to come. Reports of infection spreads make it clear that the best thing we can do to stop the spread is stick to the guidelines set out by the public health authorities. But how to make some use of the time and to do something constructive?

Over the years, I have found it a good idea to start with something practical, not requiring too much mental effort. Get the body moving. Fix something. Install something. Then, when the body has got a move on, shift to something more long-term sustainable – social contacts, letter/email writing, family reconnections, seeking out those in need – maybe write to the Premier to encourage her – she has a terrible day job right now.

It is a bit like the old *Standard Ten* I used to own. When the battery was flat, you had to get the car rolling in neutral, preferably down a hill, put in the clutch, move the car into gear and then let the clutch out so that the movement of the motor drew the fuel into the engine. Activity got the juices going.

Of course, this is not just about 'getting going'. We want to be doing something worthwhile, and for Christians that means that it has about it the marks of Christian character. Paul wrote to the church in Ephesus at a time when he saw them in difficult times and urged them to make the most of the time and understand the will of God.

We may need to 'hill start' as this COVID drags on but even the hill start committed to God can bring blessing to ourselves and to others. It is part of the offering of our lives to God, an offering that Paul says is our reasonable worship (Romans 12:1).

20

Rumours and conspiracies

The truth will make you free.
John 8:32

The deeper we get into this COVID crisis, the more we see rumours and conspiracies circulating about all sorts of things, not just to do with COVID. It is a measure of our general anxiety. So we can believe, or be tempted to believe, that COVID is a Chinese government plot to undermine the western world. Or perhaps that COVID was caused by radiation from 5G wireless technology because Wuhan had the highest concentration of 5G towers in the world. Such rumours flourish in a time of anxiety as do opinions loosely related as facts. For example, masks will make you ill.

The trouble with this atmosphere in social interactions is that it breeds distrust. I think this means for us as Christians that we should question rumours and conspiracy-like messages. Ask: how do you know that? Do you think really we should assume that our Chief Medical Officers are deliberately misleading us?

There is something quite important at stake in this. Truth in social conversations engenders trust and trust enables community life. One thing as Christians we might contribute to our society is to be well informed about the present crisis so that we can identify an ill-informed rumour or a speculative conspiracy theory.

Of course, as Christians we are people who are borne along by the open way in which God is present to us in Christ. We live that great truth. Maintaining a commitment to truthfulness in the midst of this crisis can contribute to building trust in our community and in the process make it a much better place for human flourishing.

21

Relying on God

Cast all your anxiety on him because he cares for you.
1 Peter 5:7

This week has brought us the first signs of hoped-for good news from the disastrous second wave in Victoria and also some hope from the trends in New South Wales that suggest no second wave just now. But we are far from where we were at the beginning of COVID. In the first stage, we were warned this would be a long term challenge and that we could expect subsequent waves of infections. At that time, it was hard to really believe that and so we were able to approach that prospect with some sense of confidence. We were warned things could go wrong but we hoped they would not.

Our present situation is different. We know now that a second wave can be much worse than the first. We also know in more detail that mistakes have been made and that they have contributed to the disaster in Victoria and with the *Ruby Princess* in NSW. Health workers, who are our front line warriors in this battle, are suffering serious casualties. Before our eyes Daniel Andrews and Gladys Berejiklian have aged under the stress of their responsibilities as have very many others in our community.

Some of the early Christians suffered times of persecution which challenged their faith. In our circumstances, we also face a challenge to sustain our Christian response to the struggle of our nation and of the whole world. Day in and day out, we are called to sustain such Christian virtues as humility, patience, kindness and care for others. The aging firebrand Peter offered some advice to his fellow Christians facing persecution which could well be read in the context of COVID-19. His resurrection life style looks beyond the present to make sense of the present. A point very relevant to our circumstances.

> Humble yourselves therefore under the mighty hand of God, so that he may exalt you in due time. Cast all your anxiety on him, because he cares for you. Discipline yourselves, keep alert. Like a roaring lion your adversary the devil prowls around, looking for someone to devour. Resist him, steadfast in your faith, for you know that your brothers and sisters in all the world are undergoing the same kinds of suffering. And after you have suffered for a little while, the God of all grace, who has called you to his eternal glory in Christ, will himself restore, support, strengthen, and establish you. To him be the power forever and ever. Amen.
>
> 1 Peter 5:6-11

22

Being refreshed

*Those who drink from the water that I shall give
will never be thirsty.*
John 4:14

Six months ago on Australia Day, the Victorian Health Department announced the first COVID case in Australia – a man who had just arrived from Wuhan in China. Five months ago the Prime Minister announced the COVID Emergency National Plan for what he described as a pandemic. So far there have been over 23 million cases and 808,697 deaths world-wide. In Australia, 24,811 cases and 502 deaths. Victoria is suffering a second wave that is much worse that the first. Our health authorities say we can expect more waves and no vaccine until probably late next year and even then it may not be a long-lasting vaccine.

So far, we have been able to hope for the next 'lowering of the curve' almost as if this will be the end of this crisis. No one in authority is saying any such thing. So, the idea that we can hope for an end in the near future, or after the next 'lowering' is not a reliable basis for living our lives. The trouble is we are social beings – 'herd animals'.

However, we should remember that we are not just herd animals, or just social beings. We are also individuals and we have not only individual needs such as social engagement, but we also have individual resources. Think of the Thai football players trapped in a water logged cave. They discovered personal resources they never thought they had. The history of humanity is full of such 'resource discovery' under stress. We are social beings, but we are social beings as individuals.

Christianity not only reflects that individual social aspect of our existence; it is a central part of the way God deals with us. He calls and sustains us by name as individuals and provides for us to live in interaction with others. Our lives are made up of elements of social engagement and individual action. Both aspects are vital to our living, our humanity and to our Christian existence.

For some time, we are going to live with markedly reduced social engagement. Building our hope on the next 'lowering' and the restoration of our social engagement will not be helpful or sustainable for the long run in front of us. So, we need to find those resources that belong to us in our own individual lives. For the Christian, these include prayer for ourselves and others, meditation, private reading of Scripture and helpful books or appreciating the quiet, wonder and beauty of music and art, not least the art of the natural world around us – whatever sustains our spirit and our Christian character.

When our social side is restricted, we need to nourish our inner selves.

23

Generous and kind

.. the one who bountifully sows will also reap bountifully.
2 Corinthians 9:6

Last week, I wrote about nurturing our inner spirit and made some broad suggestions including some time for meditation. One of the best resources I know is a little book by a former Archbishop of Canterbury, Michael Ramsey, *Be Still and Know*. This is from the preface.

> This book has a single theme, but its two parts are different in form. The first part is a study of the Prayer of Jesus and the understanding of prayer on St Paul, St John and the Letter to the Hebrews as well as in the story of the Transfiguration. The second part is more directly pastoral in form, and deals with sone of the practical aspects of Christian praying, with a digression on some lessons from the English Mystics of the fourteenth century and the Spanish Mystics of the sixteenth, in the belief that they speak to our contemporary world. The title *Be Still and Know* describes a recurring plea in the book that stillness and silence are of supreme importance and that the neglect of them is damaging to the Christian life.

You can buy the book online at Wipf and Stock. https://wipfandstock.com/be-still-and-know.html
Like his book, Michael was a gentle and generous spirit. Not at all self-serving or self-promoting but rather a great

encourager. In 1978, in the bookshop in Durham Cathedral, there was a book signing for two local authors of new books. Michael was in one corner of the shop and the other author diagonally opposite. Michael had a long queue waiting for him to sign his book. The other author had just a few and soon none. At one point, Michael left his place and came across the bookshop. He sat next to the other, younger author, asked to buy a copy of his book and would he please sign it for him.

Generosity of spirit and kindness not only are Christian virtues but they go a long way to foster connection and community. In a COVID time we need this both as receivers and givers. We are called to these habits by the crucified Christ whom we name as Lord.

24

Take and read

These are written so that you may come to believe.
John 20:31

Two of the most interesting characters in Christian history are Stephen Langton and Robert Stephanus. The work of both of these men is present every time you read the Bible. Stephen Langton (1150-1228), born in Lincolnshire, became a leading European scholar and, as Archbishop of Canterbury, participated in the writing of the *Magna Carta*. His significance for readers of the Bible is that he divided the text into orderly chapters instead of the arbitrary, continuous printing that had previously existed. In 1550, a French printer named Robert Stephanus (1503-1559) moved Acts from after the letters of Paul to follow the Gospels and he also introduced verses which he numbered. Almost all subsequent editions of the Bible have followed what these two men did.

Before that, people read the contents of the New Testament as a running text. The original Greek texts would not even have had any punctuation. So reading the New Testament documents by chapters, and especially verses, is a modern innovation. No doubt it is useful but it is also useful to read these texts without reference to the verses or the chapters. In fact, reading these documents without the chapters and verses is a good exercise in shaping our understanding and also our experience of these writings and their testimony to Christ.

A good way to start is with Mark because it is short and can be read within half an hour. Here is how I have done it. Find a modern English version that does not mark out the verses on the page. Bear in mind that, in the first generation, the gospels were not read off the page. A reader had the manuscript and read it out loud to the group of Christians who had gathered to hear the story. This is how most of Paul's letters addressed to churches would have been received in a church. Mark can easily be read straight off, from beginning to end. It is well written and moves along at a brisk pace. The story line is clear and is full of highlights and focal points.

Tension is marked by things like Jesus telling people not to tell others about him and warning the disciples of dangers ahead. Mark is in many ways like an Agatha Christie thriller, though there is no meeting in the living room at the end to sort it all out. You are left with the astonishment of the women at the empty tomb. Reading Mark in this way will give you a strong sense of the story line and how the main character holds the whole thing together.

You will get a sense of the narrative, which is why the gospel was written in the first place. In this way, we can come to be shaped by the story in our habits and feelings which will itself grow resilience in hard times.

25

The gift of music

... singing and making melody to the Lord in your hearts...
Ephesians 5:19

Finding it hard to escape the mundane and immediate during this time with COVID-19? Try some music framing to nurture your spirit.

The Bible begins and ends with a vision of God present with humans – walking in the garden, making his home with them. These images bracket the great Christian truth that in Jesus Christ, God is again amongst humans and restoring relationships. But, in the meantime, the song of the universe is distorted. Just as our Christian lives are formed by Jesus Christ, so also we wait patiently for the restoration of all things.

Here and now, we have some vision, some intimations of God's presence. Formed by the documents of the New Testament, we are enabled to live recognisably Christian lives, but because we are not just thinking beings, we are also deeply moved by sight and sound, and so by art and music. Some music gives us an intimation of the presence and character of God. It sets within us both deep contentment and a feeling of the divine. Such music can be a strong encouragement in sustaining our lives as Christians.

The gift of music

On my computer, I have my favourite music – Mozart, Beethoven, Bach, Sibelius, Mendelsohn, Brahms, Tchaikovsky, and all the others – with Glenn Miller playing in the café at the door, and Benny Goodman swinging the pedestrians along... Some of this music resonates with and enriches day to day life, but Mozart and Bach speak of something more sublime. Ever since Mozart wrote his extraordinary music, musicologists and also theologians have been captivated and in awe of it. There is something in it that evokes our human instinct for the sublime.

Mozart is the best example I know of music that can move a Christian beyond words and sentences to wonder and awe, peace from the God and Father of Jesus Christ. This kind of listening is a bit like meditation. It takes time and attentiveness. Mozart may not be for you. But find some music that lifts your soul and inhabit that music by regularly listening for the discovery of the peace and wonder of God.

PS On Mozart, try *Ave verum corpus*.

26

Imagination and art

*Stand up and raise your hands,
because your redemption is drawing near.*
Luke 21:28

When I was growing up, on average twice a day, I sat at the dining room table in my parents' house looking across the room at two paintings, *The Angelus* and *The Gleaners*, by the French artist Jean-Francois Millet (1814-1875). *The Gleaners* depicted three poverty-stricken peasants gathering the left-overs from the main crop. *The Angelus* portrays two peasants in the field standing to pray at the end of their work as the church bell chimed in the distance.

These images were embedded in my memory. *The Gleaners* about the grinding poverty of peasant labour in mid nineteenth century France. Over the years, it has been *The Angelus* that has become something like a computer screen saver in my mind. It speaks of these Christian folk living on the edge of social and domestic disaster being sustained under the hand of God rather than the boot of the landowner. The prayer that almost certainly Millet imagined they would be using was the Angelus.

Imagination and art

We beseech Thee, O Lord, pour thy grace into our hearts; that as we have known the Incarnation of thy Son, Jesus Christ, by the message of an angel, so by his Cross and Passion we may be brought unto the glory of his Resurrection.

This beautiful piece of art conveys a whole range of meanings, and, in this case, wonderful Christian truths of how in the ups and downs of our lives we are sustained by the outstretched hand of God in Christ. That we know the grace of God in our hearts. That we know Jesus from his birth to his cross and live in the confident hope of his and our resurrection. This is a great prayer and associated with a great piece of art.

Much great art has the capacity to reach our imaginations and hearts in a way that words cannot. We can spend time before a painting like Millet's *Angelus* taking in the image and what it tells us. Holding to such art our spirits can be sustained and lifted in trying times. Find the images that stir some Christian truth in you and embed them in your memory.

27

The face of God

He is the image of the invisible God, the firstborn of all creation.
Colossians 1:16

Recent days have seen increasing easing of restrictions as infection rates reduce. The Health Department announced that the Woollahra Local Government Area was no longer designated a 'High Risk' area and many restrictions have now been eased. So are we returning to our June level of almost no infections or will we have a Victorian experience? Epidemiologists are still very cautious and, of course, we cannot live long term cut off from the rest of the world. In NSW, we have what we have and we should be grateful for it as long as it lasts.

Our anxieties and worries may reasonably characterise how we are, but they do not define who we are. That is determined by the action of Christ in our lives. Our belonging to God is what makes us who we are. Last week, I wrote about art as a focus for sustaining our faith. In the Eastern Orthodox churches, icons are used as a focus for such meditation. The icon is, of course, not a sacred thing in itself. Rather it is a window through which we are reminded of the presence of God, a particular form of art which draws us to the sacred and beckons us more deeply into communion with our God.

In his somewhat agitated second letter to the Corinthians, Paul nailed this with consummate accuracy in defending his ministry. He refers to the light of the gospel of the glory of Christ who is the image (eikon) of God.

> For we do not proclaim ourselves; we proclaim Jesus Christ as Lord and ourselves as your slaves for Jesus' sake. For it is the God who said, 'Let light shine out of darkness,' who has shone in our hearts to give the light of the knowledge of the glory of God in the face of Jesus Christ.
>
> 2 Corinthians 4:5-6

Moses was not allowed to see the face of God on Mt Sinai but we have seen the face of God in Christ. That is who we are; and when epidemic or disturbing mood changes challenge us, that is the rock on which to stand.

28

The imitation of Christ

*Clothe yourselves with the new self,
created according to the likeness of God.*
Ephesians 4:24

October 12 in the USA is Columbus Day which celebrates the arrival of Christopher Columbus in the new world in 1492. This marked the beginning of the European era of world history. A truly momentous event. But our *Prayer Book for Australia* strikes a different note. It nominates for remembrance and celebration Elizabeth Fry, who died this day in 1845. Born into a Quaker family, Elizabeth was taken by a friend to Newgate Prison in London where she found women prisoners in desperate and degraded conditions. She spent the rest of her life working for the relief of conditions for prisoners. She visited ships in the London docks that were about to take prisoners to Australia as convicts and gave them clothing and food for their journey. Her persistent work led to changes in the law about prisons and the conditions of women.

She made a difference and in a way that marked a new beginning in human civilisation. In her time, she demonstrated – in a dramatic way – what is really important in Christian life, echoing Matthew's story of the last judgment.

> Then the king will say to those at his right hand, 'Come, you that are blessed by my Father, inherit the kingdom prepared for you from the foundation of the world; for I was hungry and you gave me food, I was thirsty and you gave me something to drink, I was a stranger and you welcomed me, I was naked and you gave me clothing, I was sick and you took care of me, I was in prison and you visited me'. Then the righteous will answer him, 'Lord, when was it that we saw you hungry and gave you food, or thirsty and gave you something to drink? And when was it that we saw you a stranger and welcomed you, or naked and gave you clothing? And when was it that we saw you sick or in prison and visited you?' And the king will answer them, 'Truly I tell you, just as you did it to one of the least of these who are members of my family, you did it to me'.
>
> Matthew 25:34-40

I am not sure if Elizabeth Fry thought those women in Newgate prison represented Christ to her. I rather think she saw their conditions with compassion and helped them. In the immediate and ordinary Jesus is revealed in Christlike actions. We may not solve the COVID vaccine or make some dramatic and great contribution to our nation or world. We will be known where it counts as we live in Christ-like fashion in our own circumstances.

That is of much greater significance in the kingdom of God than marking the beginning of the European era in world history.

29
Authentic worship

*Not everyone who says to me 'Lord, Lord'
will enter the kingdom of heaven.*
Matthew 7:21

For Bulletin production reasons, this edition of *How About This?* is being written on 4 October. I don't know where we will be on 21 October. I hope a little better off with COVID and its associated challenges. Each day in our house, we use *A Prayer Book for Australia* to say Morning Prayer together. It is a habit that reminds us of God's presence in our lives, and the lives of those for whom we pray. The collect for this week of 21 October includes the phrase 'give us pure hearts and steadfast wills to worship you in spirit and in truth'. The words allude to Jesus encounter with the Samaritan woman at Jacob's well near Sychar who challenged Jesus about the correct place to worship God. Jesus replies that place is irrelevant.

Here is the critical issue: true worshippers will worship God in spirit and truth. Worship is transformed by Jesus by being turned from where and how to the character of our worship – in spirit and truth. The truth which Jesus brings. Paul uses similar language when he sums up the behavioural meaning of that truth.

Authentic worship

I appeal to you therefore, brothers and sisters, by the mercies of God, to present your bodies as a living sacrifice, holy and acceptable to God, which is your spiritual worship. Do not be conformed to this world, but be transformed by the renewing of your minds, so that you may discern what is the will of God—what is good and acceptable and perfect.

Romans 12:1-2

So worship is how we live wherever we are; this is the worshipping of God in spirit and truth. It involves discerning God's will, what is good and acceptable and perfect, and doing it. So how we live in the ordinary daily activities of life is where we will worship God in spirit and in truth. No deed is too small nor action too great that does not fall under this rubric.

The heart of Christian faith is in what we do and how we do it.

30

Time to celebrate

Rejoice and be glad for your reward in great in heaven.
Matthew 5:12

It is now seven months since this column began and we have been through a lot in that time. We have experienced very hard times and witnessed horrific things for our neighbours in Victoria. In Australia, we seem to be getting a little control on the spread of this virus but in the rest of the world the situation is appalling. Counting per million of the population so far: *deaths* US 694, UK 658, Australia 35; *infections* US 26,598, UK 12,559, Australia 1,075.

While we seem to be doing well the global situation is quite grim and means that there is certainly more to come for us. Living with COVID means doing everything we can to control its spread while expecting some bad times to come along before a vaccine is widely administered across the world.

As a community, we can only sustain long term lock downs with superhuman effort and much pain. When infections are more controlled and we can have more freedoms to move and engage, we should take the opportunity to refresh our spirits and strengthen our communities while we can.

Time to celebrate

As Christians in the southern hemisphere, it is a time to rejoice in the spring time of the natural order. The jacarandas are already out and about throwing beauty across our streets and parks. Flowers are bursting forth and the sky is very often a beautiful blue. It reminds me of Mrs Alexander's song – 'All things bright and beautiful, all creatures great and small, all things wise and wonderful, the Lord God made them all'.

We are amongst the most fortunate on the globe with this virus – so far – and it is coinciding with Spring vitality. We have a time to refresh ourselves and our communities, to enliven our faith and trust in God, and to reach out to others in this precious intermission in our lives.

31

Keep in touch

Encourage one another and build up each other.
1 Thessalonians 5:11

This year has been a time of keeping in touch with people in different ways. Not so many close personal visits or joint activities. Fewer 'bumping into' people in the street or supermarket. More phone calls. Discovering zoom and managing it so that it is a bit more personal than just a screen image. More written correspondence by letter or email. We use what we can to sustain our social and personal contacts because they help us to continue to be the people we are, to sustain each other's well-being. As Christians, we are called to do this kind of thing. It is not just a human thing to do, it has also been a very Christian thing to do from the earliest of times.

The apostle Paul travelled a lot and in about AD 60 he found himself in gaol in Rome and wrote to two little Christian communities he had never met but whom his colleague Epaphras had established. He wrote to each church and asked them to swap letters after they had read them. His letter to Laodicea has not survived but the one to Colossae has. He begins by recalling their Christian conversion and then spells out what he prays for them: 'that they may be filled with the knowledge of God's will in all spiritual wisdom and understanding, so that you may lead lives worthy of the Lord, fully pleasing to him, as you bear fruit in every good work and as you grow in the knowledge of God'.

It is a wonderful summary of what he longs for in this little church and it is stated in such general terms that it can speak also to us as we live through these changing and challenging times. It is a picture to remember when we write, email, zoom, phone or in any way reach out to others. There will be good practical things that we need to do, but in the overall pattern of our lives, Paul's prayer for the Christians in Colossae is a wonderful model for us.

32

Daily prayer

*In everything by prayer and supplication with thanksgiving
let your requests be made to God.*
Philippians 4:6

Everyone knows that this has been a year of disruptions. The draught, the bush fires, and then COVID. Our normal patterns of life have been disrupted and changed. For some, life has been totally and disastrously changed in terms of health, work and school. In the ordinary course of living, we rely on some degree of order within which our lives flourish.

Finding that order has become a more conscious challenge this year. For Christians, this has related to such different experiences of being church and gathering for worship. We have learned about zoom church, streaming and online services which we were able to find all around the world. The Community News has taken on dimensions and value never envisaged when it was first started in February 2017 and is a wonderful help in keeping us connected.

A very powerful way Christians can retain order in their lives and grow in faith is through daily prayer. Daily prayer has been a Christian tradition for centuries. Our Prayer Book (*A Prayer Book for Australia*) introduced changes in Daily Prayer to provide for personal and family prayers. The form is simple and easily adapted for different individual circumstances. It is well worth a try – borrow a copy of the Prayer Book from the church. There are themes for Monday – The Holy Spirit, Thursday – the coming of Christ as Son of God, Friday – the Cross.

The prayers for these days begin with an appropriate text of Scripture. For Thursday, the text is Hebrews 13:15 – 'Through Christ let us offer up a sacrifice of praise to God, the fruit of lips that acknowledge his name'. This text comes in a passage that portrays Christ's death by reference to the Jewish Temple sacrifice for sins. Jesus' death on the cross brings the remission of sins into the forefront of our lives as Christians and so we offer a sacrifice of praise to God.

This is both a life-changing and a faith-sustaining truth. It is just one part of Daily Prayer in our Prayer Book. There is a lot more to discover there and regular use is good food for our souls.

33

Right or wrong

Seeking the truth in love,
we must grow up in every way into him
who is the head, into Christ.
Ephesians 4:15

Generally speaking, we don't like losing an argument or a contest, whether we are powerful or important people or we are just ordinary folk who think something is really important. We have a nice reminder of a Christian approach to this. Tuesday this week, we remember in our Prayer Book St Hilda of Whitby who died on 17 November 680. She had royal blood and was a powerful and influential woman. At the age of 30, she founded an abbey on the headland overlooking the port of Whitby on the north east coast of England.

The abbey housed both nuns and monks which was the Celtic practice. It was said of her that in all she did she exemplified Christian character and wisdom. Indeed, her virtuous life, wisdom, and unceasing care for others, no matter their social status, led to her veneration shortly after her death.

Hilda was committed to the Celtic form of Christian practice. In 663/664, a very important synod was held in the abbey at Whitby to deal with the conflict between those following the Roman tradition of the date of Easter and those who followed the Celtic date. The mercurial Wilfrid led the Roman cause and won the decision of the king who presided. The Celtic representatives left and moved to the western edges of England. Hilda, though strongly supporting the Celtic side, resolved that the king's decision was reasonably made and she should follow it. This great synod marked the eclipse of the Celtic character of the church in England.

Hilda's conduct and her action after the synod showed her belief that the church should be held together and that the date of Easter was not of such church shattering importance. Despite her conviction of the rightness of the Celtic side she placed the Christian community ahead of her judgment. It is a strong lesson for us as Christians to recognise that our personal opinions are not necessarily going to win the day in the church or in life. As with everything else in both life and the church, we belong to a higher vocation in the kingdom of God than our own opinions and the ultimate significance of every argument.

As Hilda well knew. Jesus' kingdom is not of this world.

34

Our lives before God

In him we live and move and have our being.
Acts 17:28

Once again, we are faced with such different circumstances in our nation and amongst our friends and families. In Victoria, one part of our family is coming to terms with the end of a long lockdown. In the US, another part of the family is determinedly sticking to their covenanted COVID safe regime in the 'pod' they have created with a small number of local families. These families also have young children and have agreed to hold to the same covid safe rules of conduct as they share their homes.

It is not always easy to know how to pray in such circumstances. A famous sixteenth century Swiss theologian, John Calvin (1509-1564), spoke of prayer as making God witness to our lives. We come to God and present our lives and the lives of others. It is an exercise of faith to leave with God the crux of our lives and our anxieties and hopes, our thanks and our gratitude. We absorb our lives into the hands and heart of God and thereby take to ourselves the trust and hope that God is the source of our lives present and future.

In our Anglican tradition, we have liturgical 'collects' that have a pattern that helps us in this way of living. A collect usually starts with the affirmation of some aspect of God's character and then gives voice to our hearts desire in terms of that truth. One of the collects set for this period illustrates this.

> O God,
> welcoming refuge for the outcast,
> and upholder of justice for the oppressed:
> > *maintain the hope of the poor, so that the time may soon come*
> > *when no one need want for food or shelter, and all will learn to share freely*
> following the example of your Son, who gave his very self; who now lives and reigns with you and the Holy Spirit, one God, for ever and ever. Amen.

The opening and ending of the collect point to a truth about God. The intercession in the middle shows how those praying have a role in expressing it in the here and now, the reality of the moral character of God. We become what we pray as we bring our lives before God.

35

Habits for Christian living

Rejoice always, pray without ceasing,
give thanks in all circumstances
1 Thessalonians 5:16

Exactly fifty years ago, Herbert Cole Coombes (otherwise known as 'Nugget Coombes') gave the annual Boyer Lectures on the ABC. They were published under the title of *The Fragile Pattern*.

It is just forty years since I read this book and it has had a great influenced on me. His argument was that the 'fragile pattern' is the institutions that go to make up our social life. In the language of the day, he declared that 'institutions make the man'. By which he meant that the ordered relationships that constitute our society make possible a life of freedom and value.

He knew a lot about such things. He was in charge of post-World War II national reconstruction, the first Governor of the – then government-owned – Commonwealth Bank and then first Governor of the Reserve Bank. There was hardly an aspect of national life that he did not touch. Institutions indeed shape us and help us, not only to lead a worthwhile life but also in the church to live a Christian life.

It is not a new idea. The compilers of the 1662 *Book of Common Prayer* commented on their importance and their frailty. Institutions need guarding and growing. The Royal Commission into institutional responses to child abuse showed that the institutional life of our churches had and were failing to fulfil their Christian vocation. They have since been subject to some radical surgery.

The personal version of institutions are the habits in our lives. Daily prayer is one such and quite properly a habit for many Christians, but, as our seventeenth century Anglican forebears knew, these habits need to be looked after. The habit of daily prayer is a way of supporting that prayer, not an end in itself. Jesus points to this when he tells his Jewish listeners in the 'Sermon the Mount' to go into their private room to pray, not like the scribes and pharisees for whom the form of the habit had killed the reality.

The substance of prayer to God, consciously bringing our lives into the presence of God, is what counts and what will sustain and grow our Christian life. The habit of daily prayer, the Sunday Service, or the regular House Group meeting is a support for us in growing as disciples of Christ. Habits are good when they serve the reality and values for which they exist.

36

Church as collaboration with God

For just as the body is one and has many members, and all the members of the body, though many, are one body, so it is with Christ.
1 Corinthians 12:12

This week has clearly been the week of the vaccines. They seem to be coming sooner than expected and with some confidence from the scientists. The conclusion to the pandemic – we are told – will not be immediate and there is still a long way to go, even in Australia with its repeating doughnuts. These vaccines have been the result of international collaboration between scientists, governments and private enterprises welded together by a determination to get this thing done.

History is replete with stories of the relationship between individual contribution and group interaction to achieve an agreed end. I have been reading a fascinating book on the history of the invention of computers and the internet which begins: 'most of the innovations of the digital age were done collaboratively... It's also a narrative of how collaboration and the ability to work as teams increases creativity'.

However, a lot of these people were also strong individuals. They each brought some things and they also learnt things by being together. The same is true of the social effort to deal with the virus. Health authorities advised, governments framed rules and we, the people, cooperated, and in Australia with remarkable effect.

Collaboration between individuals has been a central part of Christian faith from the beginning. In Corinth, Paul had to deal with a disorderly group of wilful individuals who thought their contribution to church was essential and the best available. He told them that their contributions were in fact 'gifts from God' and they should act with thankfulness and humility for the benefit of the others. In doing so they were to respect the gifts of others for they also were given by God.

Together, these gifts would build up a church in which Christ-like character would be growing in both individuals and in the community as a whole. This growth would be fuelled by the very character of the gospel that constituted them as Christians and a church, namely, the love of God in Christ. In the end, Paul said, we have faith, hope and love, but the greatest of these is love.

This is not a program for church life. It is a way of being church. It is how we are called to live before God as Christians in a church community.

37

Influence and responsibility

Work out your own salvation with fear and trembling,
Philippians 2:12

I often think about the relationship between influence and responsibility in its different manifestations. Think of the extreme form of this in the Christian claim that a sovereign God is shaping our lives. Paul highlighted this in his letter to the Philippians: 'Work out your own salvation with fear and trembling, for it is God who is at work in you, enabling you both to will and to work for his good pleasure'.

Think of how we all grow from new born baby when our parents control all that happens to us. Parenting is the long and multifaceted task of shaping a child's growth in a way that leads to an adult who takes responsibility for their own life. In due course, at a time not always recognised by either party, the role of parent and child changes and often, later, is reversed and a similar dynamic comes into play in a different direction. Teachers who influence others face the same challenge. How to teach in such a way that a responsible agent is formed by the interaction between teacher and student.

As a young theological student, I remember some people describing themselves as Barthians, after the famous theologian Karl Barth. Barth himself discouraged this and in a joking way declared he did not know these Barthians and he certainly was not one of them.

Coming back to Paul's letter to the Philippians, Paul wants to affirm two things – the presence of God in the life of the Christian, and the responsibility of the Christian to live and behave as a Christian. This text follows one of the greatest passages about Christ in the whole of Christian literature. It points to the mind of Christ by which the Philippians should to live. 'Do nothing from selfish ambition or conceit, but in humility regard others as better than yourselves. Let each of you look not to yourselves, but to the interests of others. Let the same mind be in you that was in Christ Jesus.'

The presence of God in our lives urges, inspires and encourages us to be and become such Christians as please God, and as reflect this mind of Christ. That means working it out, making responsible decisions and acting on them whilst being aware of the enabling presence of God as we do so.

38

Walking lightly

That... Christ will be exalted now as always in my body, whether by life or by death.
Philippians 1:20

When I was a growing up as a teenager, the phrase 'walk lightly on the earth' appeared as a way of thinking about how we should treat the environment. I did not know it at the time but it came from a group of Quakers who in 1956 started a hostel, the *Castel de Los Amigos*, in Mexico City. They gave accommodation to refugees and sought to live in a way that did least harm to the environment – hence 'walk lightly on the earth'. As has been so often in history the Quakers have been standout witnesses to Christians about how we should live in this world and in the society around us. Their phrase has become a world-wide mantra to support the planet for future generations.

As a Christian impulse, it has another dimension to it. When Paul wrote from prison to the Philippians he assured them that he was not worried by his circumstances for his ambition was that 'Christ will be exalted now as always in my body, whether by life or by death'. He sat light to his life circumstances because his life belonged to Christ. He knew that his citizenship was in heaven.

We see a similar attitude in Mary and Joseph recorded in the Christmas story. Mary and Joseph accept things as they encounter them: strange, out of place birth of a baby, no room at the inn, strange and intimidating visitors, and then threatened by cruel political danger and a long trek to Egypt. They walked lightly on the earth because their lives belonged to God.

The Quakers in Mexico City showed something of the moral character of the life of God, just as Joseph and Mary showed the relaxed acceptance of the life we have from Christ in severe and testing times. There is a message here as to how we might live moral ways in testing times.

It being the week before Christmas, I hope, dear reader, that this Christmas will bring you the blessing of a resilient trust in the Christ to whom we belong in this life and the next.

39

Resolution time and habits

*Almighty God, give us grace
that we may cast away the works of darkness
and put on the armour of light.*
From the Prayer set for the First Sunday in Advent
in the church calendar

A New Year is upon us and so we hope that it will be better for humanity and the planet than this past year has been. At this time, we are often asked if we have made any New Year's resolutions. Long ago, in youthful enthusiasm, I thought these were an unwelcome burden to lay upon myself. Later in life, facing the challenge of adult living and parenting, and learning a bit more about how our sentiments and actions are formed, I came to see some value in such things.

However, as Christians we have available to us two different time systems or calendars. The public calendar is a form of the Gregorian calendar, finalised and widely accepted in the late sixteenth century. It was a revision of the calendar authorised by Julius Caesar. It follows the rotation of the earth around the sun and thus – in practical experience – the seasons of the years: Summer, Autumn, Winter, Spring. By this calendar, then, we know that January is next and with it a new year.

The church calendar works in the same sphere as the Gregorian calendar though it does not count the years. It is based on the date of Easter and each year describes the heart of the Christian story: Jesus' life, crucifixion and resurrection. The church year begins in Advent with preparation for the Christmas celebration. Advent also points us beyond this time framed world to Jesus' kingdom which is not of this world when time as we know it now will not be part of our existence.

Time is an artefact for our living in the here and now. The Gregorian calendar helps us to plan our day and week. The seasons in the church calendar can be valuable ways to train ourselves in discipleship. These can be tools in shaping our lives as Christians as we seek to nurture the sustaining and enduring habits of living that will grow our Christian character.

40

Following Jesus

*If I want him to remain alive until I return,
what is that to you? Follow me.*
John 21:21

We have encountered some new turns in the COIVD experience. A much more contagious mutation of the virus has emerged in England and countries around the world have acted to contain this fast spreader. It has arrived in Australia and prompted strong action in Queensland and elsewhere. Some vaccines have arrived but it is now clear that availability and delivery are complicated matters. Compared with other countries around the world, we have been very fortunate with this pandemic both as to our response and our capacity to cope with its ever- changing narrative. COVID is now obviously not an event but a narrative.

Christians ought to be able to understand this way of looking at life. Our Christian life is a narrative, often requiring patience and discipline and the encouragement of a community of fellow travellers. The narrative of the Israelites in the Hebrew Bible is familiar to us and is the background from which the Christian story was born.

Christianity is also formed as a narrative. In the New Testament, what we know about Jesus is set out in the Gospel narratives. The letters are commentary on how to live a

Christian life or how to be a Christian church. At the end of John's Gospel, Jesus asks Peter if he loves him. It is a testing and difficult exchange. At the end, Jesus simply say to Peter, 'Follow me'. Then follows an exquisite exchange, hinting at currents of jealousy and comparison that arise in groups of people, in this case among Jesus' disciples.

Peter turned and saw that the disciple whom Jesus loved was following them. (This was the one who had leaned back against Jesus at the supper and had said, 'Lord, who is going to betray you?') When Peter saw him, he asked, 'Lord, what about him?' Jesus answered, 'If I want him to remain alive until I return, what is that to you? Follow me.' The COVID narrative is the context of our current life. The narrative of our following Jesus is the substance of our life by which we are, and are seen to be, Christians.

41

Heroes to inspire

Welcome Epaphroditus then in the Lord with all joy, and honour such people.
Philippians 2:29

Next week, we celebrate Australia Day. There will be differences to the celebrations this year because of the COVID rules. Nonetheless, there will be celebrations and the Australian of the Year will be announced. I have always admired this part of the celebration, even though there is a dark side to the date. I remember when the award was started in 1960 – I was a young cadet engineer at what is now Sydney Water.

Each state or territory nominates one candidate. Three main criteria are used when considering nominees: demonstrated excellence in their field; significant contribution to the Australian community and nation; and an inspirational role model for the Australian community. Generally, the elected person gains widespread public support for the obvious reason that these criteria are in themselves things we naturally admire.

The last – an inspirational role model for the Australian Community – is interesting because, as we in NSW know, in the horrific bush fires of last year, we looked forward to hearing Shane Fitzsimmons giving us the latest updates on the fires and helping the state to get through the disaster. Similarly, last year Brendan Murphy, the Commonwealth Chief Medical Officer at the time, helped us feel that decisions were in good hands. Not surprisingly, both are nominees this year. There are five women amongst the eight nominees, an increase on previous years, and the first indigenous doctor ever nominated. These are heroes all, who have worked in aboriginal health, disability issues, sexual abuse and with homeless people.

Pope John Paul II created 482 saints in the Roman Catholic church as compared with 300 in the previous 600 years. We have saints' days in our church – on average several each week. We don't always notice them because they come on week days. The saints are Christians who have been heroes of the faith past and present.

Heroes of our country who are nominated as Australians of the Year provide role models for our better selves. Honouring heroes of the faith also reminds us of the better selves we are called to be in our Christian communities. We should probably know more about them. They can inspire us.

42

Paul as hero

For it is not those who commend themselves that are approved, but those whom the Lord commends.
2 Corinthians 10:18

In our church calendar this week, we celebrate the festival of the conversion of Paul the apostle. We probably have a vision of Paul as a writer of letters, sometimes complicated even convoluted. Sometimes revealing the assumptions of his day in his advice to his churches, perhaps without noticing, as we also sometimes do. At least one of his contemporaries found Paul's letters hard going (2 Peter 3:16).

Paul was born in Tarsus and was a Roman citizen by birth. He was educated there and also in Jerusalem as a Jewish Rabbi. He worked for the High Priest's Council for a time. Energetic and smart, he was a zealot for the cause of Jewish orthodoxy. He became a Christian and turned his zeal into service of his new risen master. The only description we have of his appearance comes from about one hundred years after his death and states that he was 'a man small in size, bald-headed, bandy-legged, well-built, with eyebrows meeting, rather long-nosed, full of grace'. He died, probably in Rome, as a prisoner for his faith.

His letters and the stories of him in the Acts of the Apostles show a man of enormous energy and patience – mostly.

He started churches across the towns and cities around the Aegean Sea and kept in touch with them by visits and letters. These letters were written to answer questions, enquire how they were going and always to encourage them.

Sometimes, these churches were a bit of a trial, like the Corinthians who seemed to have difficulty absorbing quite basic Christian values. In Philippi, there appear to have been some difficult group interactions; in Thessalonica, external pressures and anxieties about aspects of their new faith. Through it all, Paul shows commitment to the people, patience with their troubles and consistency in encouraging them to follow Jesus with faith, hope and love.

Some of the things he wrote are hard, complex, uncomfortable and some very much of their time. But he is a saint from the first generation, worthy to be amongst our gallery of heroes to honour and from whom to learn.

Here is the prayer for his day from our *Prayer Book*.

Almighty God, whose blessed apostles Peter and Paul glorified you in their death as in their life: grant that your Church, inspired by their teaching and example, and made one by your Spirit, may ever stand firm upon the one foundation, Jesus Christ your Son our Lord, who is alive and reigns with you, in the unity of the Holy Spirit, one God, now and for ever. Amen.

43

Difference and diversity

Now there are varieties of gifts, but the same Spirit.
1 Corinthians 12:4

Just over one hundred years ago, a famous American social psychologist, Leon Festinger, was born in New York City. He developed theories of group dynamics and social networks which today are part of the way we think about social life. He provided a framework for understanding an important principle in human flourishing which had been long known by Christians but often forgotten. We can flourish in contexts of difference and diversity. We can stultify in sameness and uniformity.

Of course, either of these can be too much of a good thing at times. When Paul was starting churches in Greece and Asia Minor, he encouraged two things that touch on this. Within the local community, there were different talents, skills and capacities for the good of everyone in the community. Paul called these capacities 'gifts' in recognition that they were gifts from God and therefore should be used for purposes that were 'God-shaped'. That is why love determined the way these differences were to be exercised.

He also extended that principle to the relations between the churches which did not shape their community life in the same way. These groups similarly benefit from interacting with each other because they are saved by the same Christ and live to serve the same Christ. Thus, he recommended one church to follow the example of another, he organised a collection among the churches for the poor in Jerusalem and he recommended a member of one church to another church.

A lot has happened since Paul's time in the way churches are formed socially but these two principles still warrant attention. Nurture and use the gifts that God has given you. Nurture the interaction between your group and others. In both processes, we become open to the possibility of both learning something and being encouraged in our faith.

44

Things by the wayside

While they were talking and discussing,
Jesus himself came near and went with them,
but their eyes were kept from recognising him.
Luke 24:15

This past week has had its moments. The Victorian Premier called an emergency press conference in the very early hours of the morning to announce a COVID case and some new measures, but assured Victorians not to panic. What was going on here? Surprisingly, we heard that China and Russia had started exporting millions of their home-grown vaccines to developing countries, marking the possibility of a significant breakthrough in controlling the virus in these countries.

I had my own small example on Friday. I had to arrange a medical appointment and got the message machine saying they would call me back. Ten minutes before closing time, I missed their call because I fumbled my iPhone. I called back quickly but the message machine now told me they were closed for the weekend. Not happy!

Things don't always happen just as we would like and a preoccupation with the immediate may mean missing the more important. Think of the two disciples on the road to Emmaus who were preoccupied with the tragedy in

Jerusalem and the events of Jesus' crucifixion and how the women of their company had found the tomb empty. They talked at length about the things they had experienced in Jerusalem. Then a stranger joined them on the road. They really did not pay much attention to him. They simply blurted out their story. In fact, they were completely taken up with their own experience. It dominated their minds and their conversation. No social enquiry about who he was and where he was going. Even when the stranger gave them such a surprisingly informed interpretation of the events in Jerusalem, they simply focused on their story. When they stopped for a meal, they still did not identify their conversationalist, even in the light of the room. But then he broke bread in a familiar way and they immediately recognised that this was Jesus.

We should walk through life quietly and with our peripheral vision turned up. We might see some interesting and important things that God has put along the wayside.

45

On truth-telling

But I say to you, Do not swear at all.
Matthew 5:34

The tenure of Donald Trump was full of challenges about truth-telling. Fake news, liar, non-truth, alternative truth were words often heard on the airwaves from all sides. The issue was not so much the nature of truth in some ultimate or philosophical sense. Rather, it was about truth telling in social life, in personal terms in our interaction with each other.

Jesus set the bar very high. 'You have heard that it was said to those of ancient times , "You shall not swear falsely, but carry out the vows you had made to the Lord". But I say to you, Do not swear at all ... Let your word be "Yes, yes" or "No, no"; anything more than this comes from the evil one' (see Matthew 5:33-17). This simple honesty highlights how important speech and trust are in our social relations. Jesus' injunction on oaths is directly related to his strong attacks on hypocrisy. Hypocrisy and lack of truth in speech both undermine the trust that is essential to open, reliable, social relations.

When I was in a public office in the church, I was sometimes asked directly about something of which I was aware but which was completely confidential. In our ordinary social relations, we can find ourselves in this kind of situation. How to answer honestly is not always easy. I have found it best simply to say politely, 'I rather think that touches on matters that are confidential for those involved' – or something like that. I have observed that people whom we know to be honest and straightforward are also straightforward in answering. Furthermore, they generally are also more sensitive in asking things that might involve confidentiality for others.

Honesty in conversation, not decorating with an oath or recommendation – let your yes be yes and your no be no – is a talent and a habit worth cultivating. Not only so, it is a recommendation that comes from an excellent source.

46

Imaginative concern

But a Samaritan while travelling came near him;
and when he saw him, he was moved with pity.
Luke 10:33

It has been fascinating to experience the different ways in which our political leaders have appealed to us in the COVID time. Mask wearing has been generally portrayed in terms of self-interest – it will protect you; quarantine – it's the rule and you must do it to protect others; social distancing – to prevent the spread. There is regularly an interplay between self interest and concern for the other.

Two men whose works I have found deeply interesting over many years are Jean Jacque Rousseau (1712-1778) and Adam Smith (1723-1790). Smith lived and worked in Glasgow, Rousseau in Geneva and France. Rejecting the radical individualism of his day, Smith argued that we can only share someone else's feeling and thoughts by an act of creative imagination. It was the only way to have any feeling for the suffering of another and that was necessary for our own humanity.

Rousseau told the story of a man walking through the woods and seeing another person injured and in pain, he immediately had pity on him, and – in that moment, Rousseau says – society was born and the walker gained his humanity.

All of the experiments and videos we have been shown about wearing face masks demonstrate that the mask limits the spread of viral aerosol from the person wearing the mask. In other words, mask wearing is not a selfish act to protect yourself so much as an altruistic act to protect others.

For the Christian, that altruism is driven because Christ has first loved us. Just as Smith and Rousseau show humanity in terms of personal imaginative concern, so also Christ's love for us shapes us as creative, imaginative people.

47

Richard Johnson – chaplain in hard times

What shall I render unto the Lord for all his benefits toward me?
Psalm 116:12 (KJV)

Early in the morning of 3 March 1788, at the point where Bligh and Hunter Streets now intersect, Richard Johnson preached the first Christian sermon in the new colony of New South Wales. He preached on the text Psalm 116:12 – 'What shall I render to the Lord for all his benefits toward me?' All in the colony were commanded to attend. One person reported to his family in England that it was a good sermon. The text of the sermon has not survived.

Johnson was not a commanding presence. Even his patron William Wilberforce, described him as 'very little acquainted with the world'. The head of the NSW Corps despised him, but an unidentified convict reported on his work very differently.' I believe few of the sick would recover if it were not for the kindness of the Revd Mr Johnson whose assistance out of his own stores makes him the physician both of soul and body'. Johnson was an evangelical. Not a puritan, or reformed evangelical, but, like his contemporaries, an evangelical in the mould of continental pietism.

In 1794, he published an address to the inhabitants of the colony in which he encouraged his readers on the importance of Bible reading, church attendance and prayer.

These are the marks of an earlier evangelical faith, one which I remember from my youth. It is very similar to the advice about guidance of Andrew Murray, a hero of evangelical piety in the nineteenth century, 'What do the Scriptures say, what do the brethren say, what does the Spirit say'.

That advice has been an enduring approach in my own life from the time I read them over sixty years ago. But notice that this piety was not socially passive. Johnson was remembered as kind and active in the welfare of the distressed and unwell in the colony. Johnson's sermon is specially remembered today in our *Australian Prayer Book* as from a saint and hero whom we can honour. He is indeed a person to learn from.

48

Moral choices and faith

> *He has told you, O mortal, what is good;*
> *and what does the Lord require of you but to do justice,*
> *and to love kindness, and to walk humbly with your God?*
> Micah 6:8

A year ago, at the height of the COVID crisis, we bunkered down and looked for some relief from isolation and anxiety. Over the horizon we hoped for a vaccine that might fully solve our problems. Infection rates came down and then vaccines come on line earlier than hoped but now there are supply problems and commercial contracts between our government and a European manufacturing company are in difficulties. The EU has provided its member countries with the power to divert vaccines to their use at home if they were urgently needed. This means that supplies intended for Australia won't be coming from that source yet.

Clearly, this is not just a commercial question but also a moral question. As a nation, we are in a much better position with infection rates than Italy. Morally, it seems clearly reasonable that they should have some priority. Happily, we are beginning to manufacture a vaccine here and so we will not be significantly disadvantaged. But the manufacturer did not keep their contract. Both governments here and in Europe re-asserted the right to re-direct vaccines intended for elsewhere and also the responsibility of companies to honour contracts.

Moral questions are not always, actually not often, straightforward. That is also true of choosing how to act as Christians. What is the Christian thing to do in the here and now is not always clear and we may sometimes realise in retrospect that we got it wrong. In fact, the idea of perfection is a dangerous and unchristian ideal.

The Christian ideal is to live by faith. That means not just leaving things in God's hands as we follow Jesus. It also means living as best we can and – knowing our weaknesses to do so – in humility before God. Living by faith is more intuition than calculation and measurement. Over the long term, that is why we should strengthen our intuitions to shape them with Christian values so that when we call on them they will give a ready help.

49

Reflecting on our Christian narrative

Jesus said to him, 'If it is my will that he remain until I come, what is that to you? Follow me!'
John 21:22

This week, it is just three months since non-Australian citizens from China were banned from entering Australia, while in Australia, we had five cases of COVID-19. In that three months, we have gone to the brink with this pandemic and hopefully we are turning back. It has been an amazing story, a narrative of horror and wonder as people responded, politicians put ideology aside and we learned that we had a Chief Medical Officer named Brendan Murphy. He became a more prominent figure than presumably he had ever imagined would be the case and, thankfully for us, he was up to the task.

This week, we have had in total just under 6,848 cases and 96 deaths. While new cases have dropped dramatically, they bumped up during the week.

We each have our own narrative of this disaster. Confined to home except for essential things, testing, physical distancing, the extraordinary toilet paper panic and the dramatic disruption of routines for everyone.

The absence of some sense of our place in a narrative is seriously disorienting. Even, what day is it today?? No matter how relaxed we are, some order is essential to our lives.

More than that, in the longer term, having some sense of a personal narrative is also vital to our well-being. I recently had the experience of a significant disruption of a part of my own story that had shaped my memory and my sense of who I was. This change in the narrative turned out to be a significant turning point in my own story and consequently who I thought I was and as a consequence how I thought about how I live.

As Christians, our narrative is filled with the presence of God. The presence of God is not just a parallel narrative, or even a sub plot to some other main story line. It is the warp and woof that gives our story meaning. In our present circumstances, we would do well to give some attention to our own personal narrative in terms of our belonging to the narrative that is given to us in Jesus Christ. One way to do that is, in total honesty, to bring our life in its present condition before God. Not to ask for something, but rather to meditate and reflect. Make God witness to how and where we are.

Sharing with God the narrative we are living with encourages us in our Christian life.

50

St Patrick's Breastplate

*I bind unto myself today
The power of God to hold and lead.*

It is exactly one year since I wrote the first of these features *'How About This?'*. They have been written weekly ever since. It has been a most enjoyable experience for me and mostly quite fun – although a weekly deadline is a stern taskmaster. I have decided to take a break so this will be my last for a while. I thank Stuart for the invitation to write the column, Marion for her kind editorial work, and you, dear readers, for your kind responses. I take my leave with a certain sadness.

Since today is St Patrick's Day in our church calendar, I thought the Irish saint was a nice note on which to finish this series. I remember Louise and I had a holiday in Ireland that included a road trip around the Ring of Kerry. It is beautiful country. There are bronze-age stone castles but smaller stone circles that were the remains of monastic centres and churches also caught our attention. Fifteen hundred years old, they are the remnants of small churches and monastic places where Christian faith had been maintained and Christian learning fostered.

Early Irish Christianity was quite monastic in form, a tradition that had been started by Patrick towards the end of the fifth century. Patrick did not leave lengthy writings.

St Patrick's Breastplate

He was a simple man, not learned and very conscious of his failings. But he is a great Christian for his life of faith.

I leave with you two quotations that speak to me of the steadfast faith of this Irish saint.

From his *Confession*:

> So I want to give thanks to God without ceasing. He frequently forgave my lack of wisdom and my negligence, and more than once did not become very angry with me, the one who was meant to be his helper. I was not quick to accept what he showed me, and so the Spirit prompted me. The Lord was merciful to me a thousand thousand times, because he saw in me that I was ready, but that I did not know what I should do about the state of my life.

From his *poem on faith*. This is in our church hymn books as *Patrick's Breastplate* and it is my prayer for you all.

> I bind unto myself today
> The power of God to hold and lead,
> His eye to watch, his might to stay,
> His ear to hearken to my need.
> The wisdom of my God to teach,
> His hand to guide, his shield to ward,
> The word of God to give me speech,
> His heavenly host to be my guard.

www.ingramcontent.com/pod-product-compliance
Lightning Source LLC
Chambersburg PA
CBHW011317080526
44588CB00020B/2744